Twisted

Dedication

Clint and Crystal Thurmon,
I was a house wife who dreamed of becoming an author,
And then you made me your co-author for the Superi Series.
You gave me the opportunity to share my poetry with the world.
You made my dreams come true, and in the process, you became
Cherished friends.

Copyright © 2016 by Christina R. Williams.

Library of Congress Control Number: *2016934583*

ISBN: Softcover 978-0-9970364-7-3
eBook 978-0-9970364-8-0

All rights reserved. No part of this book may be reproduced or transmitted in any form or by any means, electronic or mechanical, including photocopying, recording, or by any information storage and retrieval system, without permission in writing form the copyright owner.

This is a work of fiction and / or personal feelings. Names, characters, places, and incidents either are the products of the author's imagination or are used fictionally, and any resemblance to any actual persons, living or dead, events, or locales is entirely coincidental.

To order additional copies of this book, contact publisher:
Superi LLC.
www.superillc.com

Twisted

A Collection of Poems

By Christina R. Williams

Table Of Contents

Introduction

The hardest to tell

Terror Within	5
Daughter mine	6
It Must End	9
Monsters	10
From the Ashes	11
Growing Up Too Fast	12
Cowboy Up	14
I Am Who I Was Made	16

Where Fear Doth Dwell

Fearful State	19
Hidden Pain	20
What Happens When	21
Broken	22
Two Faces	24
Questions Without Answers	26

Where Hate Doth Rise

I Wish I Could Tell You	31
Secret Thoughts	32
Consuming Hate	33

Where Love Abides

Twisted Truth 37
Chainless Prison 38
A War Lost 40
Troubled Waters 41
Beyond What Was 42
Cherished Memory 44
So Much Left Unspoken 46
Blind Eyes Wide Open 48
Love Unattained 49
Awakening Desire 50
Stolen 51

Where Cruelty Lives

Oil and Water 55
I'm Not in Your Image 56
Betrayal of Blood 58

Where It All Ends

The Ocean Rolls 61
The Wind 62
Where the World Ends 63

And Despite What Was

As Her Mother 67
Liars Made 68

Conclusion

Introduction

If you are one who seeks sweet solace in soothing words of poetry this book is not for you. For within its pages lies fear and hate, love and loss, bitter betrayal, and victory that comes at great cost. So much of its content is truth that the telling of it becomes almost unbearable, but to be released from the past has been my journey, and now I am free.

The Hardest to Tell

Terror Within

How strange that a world so full of vibrant beauty,
Also holds the darkest of terrors within her shadow.
Stranger still, is knowing even greater nightmares,
Hide behind the brightest lights.

Daughter Mine

"Daughter mine draw near my side. I would give of myself to thee."
An excited youth comes bursting forth smiling delightedly.
"Tis my pleasure, no, tis my joy to draw ere close to you."
A slender hand upon beating hearts seals a vow betwixt the two.
"Trust I take, but trust I give; a gift given and so received."
Cold stone, meets awe filled wonder, and by it, innocence is deceived.
"Daughter mine lend thy ear for wisdom I would impart."
With trepidation the female waits for her mother's words to start.
"Family before self," she says, "family before all else."
"Why does gaining wisdom, mother, cause one to lose their self?"
"Selfishness is not of God, and silence the price we must pay,
To keep our secrets locked within, and the outside world at bay."
In the night comes a caller, a quiet knocking on the door,
A different gentleman creeping in; one different than before.
She cannot stomach to inquire, as to why he is there,
But leads him steadily instead to her mother's sinful lair.
She never looks upon their faces. She never asks their name.
The years have proven only that the morrow will bring the same.
"Daughter mine, thou knowest what I have need of so desperately,
Yet mine physician feels I've used what was given erroneously."

"My ailments differ from your own, therefor how can I be of aide?
Please ask me not to lie for you, I would be so much ashamed."
"Family before self," she says. "Trust that I know what is best.
And speak not to me of painless shame, and put your fears to rest.
The world has come against, both my tired body and weary soul.
What once was found most beautiful has grown so quickly old.
The callers come no more, you see, for they seek a maiden's kiss.
But coin I need to supply my hourly dose of sweetest bliss.
I beseech thee, daughter mine, lend your aide in this my darkest hour.
No other can supply the antidote to my pain, but tis within your power."
"Mother, ask me not to sacrifice what small piece of me yet remains.
You have taken all from me, save this sickly body and empty name.
The lies and deceit like cancer; have I not kept your secrets well,
Though the keeping has placed me within a life of hell?
Ask me not to do this thing for my mind would be the same no more.
Will thou not let me retain a measure of pride, lest I myself deplore?"

Resist she did. Sorcery stole her strength. She could taste it upon her tongue.

The callers did come, and coin for her mother made, the cost upon her young.

"Daughter mine, thou must calm thyself for the ordeal you feared is o'er."

Bruised and bloody, the female stoically replies, "I am your daughter no more.

I am but a slave, an unwilling pawn in a game that seeks to devour me.

I am but a captive of a one sided vow. Trust the cage and guilt the key."

It Must End

I wonder what you saw when you looked upon me. So weak was I when still you traversed amongst the living.

Tossed to and fro by the softest of whispering winds; the slightest shifts in the sands of life hindering my steps; timidly trembling through each hour.

What a disappointment I must have been.

Your demised changed my reality, as if waking from a dream, but the nightmare remained; the danger encompassing.

The monsters real, and you...the one who drew me into the heart of the beast escaped into the cold embrace of death, and left me to face life alone.

I am your equal in the strength now.

I face the monsters daily. I have become the encompassing danger. I am the one! I have become the nightmare. I embody it.

I have taken the fear of it; the pain of it, within myself so no other will suffer as I have suffered. In this...I am your better.

At long last I can say

I am finished. I have won, and when I draw my last breath the nightmare will end.

And those I leave behind will never know of the world in my mind that you created and I destroyed.

Monsters

I will stand for that which is right.
As a child I would often say.
But though I tried with all my might.
I couldn't stand against the evil of the day.
For the darkness was cloaked in the guise of good.
I couldn't see passed the rose colored glass.
Until at last my conscience no longer read as it should.
And when the monsters were revealed, I but cried, "Alas".
Right and wrong, like good and bad, only one can see.
Monsters do not look upon themselves as such.
Each heart and mind deciphers conscience differently.
And as to admitting sin, saints don't admit to much.
So in the grey I choose to live my life.
In the grey I take my battle stance.
I will face the monsters and ensuing strive.
In the grey I will beckon them, come, let us dance.

From the Ashes

Our mother died before her time,
Pills the culprit, pain the crime.
Three children wept, lost and alone,
Abandoned before her body was cold.
Big brother buried his sorrows deep,
Liquor to cope and liquor to sleep.
Little brother built walls within,
A self-made cage that trapped him in.
Like shattered glass, I did fall,
Guilt my personal wrecking ball.
Years have passed, no peace to find,
For those she twisted and left behind.
Little brother still hurts too much,
And liquor is still big brother's crutch.
In silence I wear my guilt and shame,
Where it will go with me to the grave.
Some say that we have hearts of stone,
They are those who do not know.
Cold as ice, but we do rise,
From the ashes of our mother's lies.

Growing Up to Fast

I think about it now and then,
About the way things might have been.
Did you ever listen?
Did you even try?
Why could you never hear my broken hearted cries?
A little girl watches her mother walk out the door,
And she prays for the strength to endure,
As little brother's tears do fall,
And he asks the question, why?
She gathers him close, but has no answer that will suffice.
A teen age girl watches her mother leave again.
Is it work, is it pills, or is it just another man?
Little brother home from school
He says, I needed mom today.
Sister says come here, I'll make it right some way.
A woman stands before her mom, and says, go ahead and leave.
The hurt you've caused is beyond belief.
Little brother's standing there,
Quiet, hurt, and sad.

He says, "Mom I don't need you now. I guess I never have."
I think about it now and then,
About the way things might have been,
If ever you had listened,
If ever you had tried,
But when last you left us, it was because you'd died.

Cowboy Up

He was five the day his mother said goodbye.
Only five years old when she left him behind.
He didn't cry.
All he said was it was time to Cowboy Up.
Not long after his daddy said he had to go.
He sent him back to mama, though he cried, no.
Don't, make me go.
His daddy said it was time to Cowboy Up.
By sixteen the streets were his to call home.
His friends were few, and they knew they were alone.
So, he held on.
When times grew tough, that's when he said, Cowboy Up.
He remembers the blood was red when he died.
His flesh was cold, as he held him, his eyes wide.
Then he cried.
All he could say was it was time to Cowboy Up.
In too deep there was nowhere for him to hide.
Hope was lost, though he managed to survive,
Without pride.
He said it was time to Cowboy Up.
He got out, though the scars they remain.

To his horror, to his terror, to his shame.
Oh God the pain.
But he said it was time to Cowboy Up.
When your back is against the wall.
And the cards are stacked to ensure your fall.
When the only choice is to give your all.
Cowboy Up.

I Am Who I Was Made

Despite the years still you play,
Upon my mind like a plague.
One of confusion, of sorrow and hate,
Where prayer fails, and hope abates.
Yin and Yang I wish we were,
For within our blood lies a curse.
Twin actions reveal, as time has told,
The absence of balance, makes youth old.
The eternal embrace of death so cold,
Is not strong enough your hate to hold.
You tare asunder; you rip in two,
Till what is left of me....is you.
What strife we cause to befall ourselves,
As we struggle to undo,
Deeds wrought by another's hands,
To others as to you.
The guilt placed upon our minds...
The shame we feel inside...
We tell ourselves it's not our blame...
Our reflection says we lie...

Where Fear Doth Dwell

Fearful State

Fear is such an ugly thing that slowly infects the soul with a cruel anxiety that makes a maiden's heart grow old. It sneaks up from behind you, striking like a snake, like venom running through your veins draining precious strength. A voice inside your head screams, just don't let it show. If we smile, and keep on going, maybe they will never know. But the fear just keeps growing, like a raging storm, and lost in the violent winds you can't find yourself any more. Life keeps moving forward, and swiftly passes you by, while you're still locked inside your fear, and inwardly you cry. You can't fight this emotion, which is just as strong as hate, so you embrace your anxious destiny. You accept your fearful state.

Hidden Pain

Just when I think I'm strong enough,
To leave my cruel past behind,
Past becomes present, terror erupts,
Catching me unprepared and blind.
I bury the pain deep in my gut.
Build my barrier thick, build it high.
I refuse to stay in this insufferable rut.
I'm okay, I'll survive, I'm alive.
I reign in my panic, racing heart control.
Put my masking smile in place.
I've been here before, I can do this alone.
This isn't the first monster I've faced.
Broken bones and battered skin.
The spray of my blood with its rusty scent.
How long this time will it take to mend?
No matter, I'll not relent?
With relief I waken from dark memory,
Though the shadows lurk behind.
I tuck away all the horror I've seen,
In search of peace of mind.

What Happens When......

What happens when the heart dies? Not physically of course, but when it can no longer emotionally help you find your way. What happens when your conscience can no longer be heard? Does evil take over what once may have been a good soul? And if so what happens when the soul dies too? When nothing is left but a vast empty space that at one time had been a person. When you can no longer smile for you have forgotten how, and you can no longer feel joy, because the despair is as thick as glue running rampant through your veins. What happens when you wake up one morning and you realize that you are just a machine? Going through the motions waiting on the day when you will be blessed with the final nothingness.

Broken

I'm broken and they cannot see…
I cannot breathe.
My heart races ahead.
Panic snapping at my heels.
Depression like a mountain.
I can't get out of bed.
Wish they could know how it feels…
This anxiety that kills.
Every day the same.
The price that I pay.
I pray and I seek.
Though lost is the way.
Their malic I cannot conceive…
It eats at me.
Love is not enough.
Respect dissipates.
Why are those I cherish.
All about the hate?
Empty words suffocate my will…
How am I to deal?
How much can I take,

Of spiteful choices spit in my face,
Or of the silence he holds,
For his own sake?
I'm coming apart at the seams.
Hear my screams!
See my tears,
See my pain.
Before I am lost,
To selfish gain.
I cannot breathe.
I'm broken and they cannot see.

Two Faces

Why do you deny who you really are?
Such secrets you bury to hide your scars.
The cost is your freedom and yet you choose,
To allow your life to become your noose.
You come alive within your dreams,
But die inside when darkness leaves.
When dawn breaks and you return,
To quietly endure and yearn,
For more than you are willing to claim,
Unable to reach beyond your shame.
A wild spirit cannot be tamed,
And passion worries not for blame.
The scars you bare have left you raw,
But they do not have to cost you all.
Choose instead to cast off the lie,
That marks you meek inside.
Embrace the reflection of your soul,
So the whole world can know,
That within the shell from which you dwell,
Is a woman who has survived hell.
Two facets of a whole divided cannot stand,

And you must accept yourself to understand
For good or bad, for gain or ill,
You are forever yourself still.
Scared and stained you maybe,
But you alone can set you free,
From the guilt you've claimed not your own,
To rise from the ashes to stand alone,
Strong and proud and free from shame,
To gain the life that's yours to claim.

Questions without Answers

Are we to be or not to be?
Famous words with many meanings.
Like waking up too fast,
Wondering if you're still dreaming.
Like having a bad day,
Saying tomorrow will be better.
No matter how bad it is,
It can't stay bad forever.
But what if there is no tomorrow?
What if there is no today?
What if we are only dreaming,
Of this world in disarray?
What should happen if we awake,
To a world of blackness and void?
Or if where utopia was to be,
We are handed a river Styx coin?
Is it really hypocrisy,
To ask questions such as these?
Answers that can't be found,
But my mind they would appease.
Maybe we are or have been,

Or perhaps will never be.
Death may reveal darkness only,
And only nothing we may see.
But whoever holds the answers,
They may never choose to share.
So let not existence be everything,
Put your worries to greater cares.
Are we to be or not to be,
Is the question we often have?
Though the only answer I can find,
Is one that causes me to laugh.

For
Questions without answers are worth nothing.

Where Hate Doth Rise

I Wish I Could Tell You

I can't believe the words I hear,
Spewing from your lips.
I try to hold back the tears,
Though I feel my heart as it rips.
How wrong you are about me,
You will never know.
My pain you'll never see,
For I'll never let it show.
Souls' cold and black,
I am not to blame.
The truth you sorely lack,
Though answers you proclaim.
For malice that infects,
You spread like a plague.
And what is right you reject,
As hypocrisy becomes your name.

Secret Thoughts

I have all that I need,
        but my wants go untouched.
I feel guilty for my greed,
        but I'm not asking much.
I want respect as a mother,
        but want the woman to show.
I want to be who I am,
        but want no one to know.
I'm a walking contradiction,
        and I hate the way that feels.
I desire to be a good person,
        but that my passive fate seals.
I want to feel alive,
        but settle for not feeling dead.
I want to be heard,
        but keep my lips sealed instead.
Don't rock the boat,
        And don't disturb the quiet flow.
For I am but a house wife,
        and this the only life I know.

Consuming Hate

From grace I have fallen,
For one cannot enter in,
A place of promised peace,
When rage rolls within.
Your presence a constant succor,
That feeds this growing hate,
And like any mortal disease,
It refuses to abate.
Such sorrow fills my soul,
For what it is I've lost,
For tears cannot ease,
The pain you have wrought.
My reflection is a blatant lie,
As is the smile you see,
For though I have survived,
I have ceased to be.

Where Love Abides

Twisted Truth

Speaking the truth, the lies spill forth through twisted words and manipulation.

I say so much, while saying nothing at all, and blame it on your lack of communication.

Forth coming to a fault I lay the truth at your feet, and dare you to call me out.

With obvious clues, and unsubtle hints, I scream for you to see what I'm about.

Fear claws at my heart while excitement speeds its pace, as I wait for the conclusion.

The moment when our friendship dies, as clarity clears away your delusions.

Life is not simple, our paths are not clear, and love is not what we often perceive.

Love is the choice made every day, and in believing its perfect, ourselves we deceive.

Life is a book full of chapters to read, and every day we turn to another page.

Our story is done, a new chapter to begin, where my desire is freed from its cage.

This is not your fault, I take full blame, for I'm the one saying I'm through.

But please believe my lying lips when I say, I never meant to hurt you.

Chainless Prison

Burdened by things beyond her control,
Buried in secrets that had n'er been told,
A youth was made old before her time,
Shame her punishment for an uncommitted crime.
Love but a figment of wild cast dreams,
And peace an unreachable, unobtainable thing,
But then death did reach, her oppressor to take,
And from her hell she did wake.
She then did hide within a hardened cocoon,
Until time sufficient had succored her wounds,
And when at last her story was told,
It began, "No matter now, what happened long ago."
With remaining pride, she spoke of pain,
Endured for another's selfish gain.
She spoke of her mother, of sickness, and lies,
But as the rape spilled forth raw tears she cried.
It was the ultimate betrayal, for her mother was there,
Watching as it happened, but cast it off without care.
Pills were her goal though her young paid the price,
Her body and mind made sacrifice.
Why, she'd asked, and her mother did reply,

Speak not to others of what I will deny,
And so until now her secrets she'd kept,
Drowning in tears that could not be wept,
"A victim I am not," she said, "but one who has survived,"
Love stirred when he then, so sweet, replied, "You're right,"
His words gave her courage, and so, she did dare,
To offer her heart to the one who'd seen it bare,
And her wild cast dreams were captured,
By his words was her spirit enraptured,
When on one knee he asked her, to be his wife,
And to share the next chapter of his life.

A War Lost

Words flow like nectar sweet,
But bitter becomes the taste,
When what comes forth from parted lips,
To fragile love lays waste.
From the promise of redemption,
Hope eternal springs,
But when all vows are broken,
Shattered becomes the dream.
Then we must wake to reality,
And leave behind such foolish quests,
As to search for what cannot be found,
Within another's breast.
Love has proven my adversary,
Desire the pyre upon which I burn.
Your heart the ice I could not thaw,
Your mind what I could not turn.
Many battles have I fought,
But the war is finally lost.
I am the ashes that remain.
My heart was the cost.

Troubled Waters

I heard the words, can I try something with you, and my heart leapt within my chest. Your voice instilled a curiosity, and it overruled my better judgment. From deep inside came an unknown sense of courage that allowed me to speak of my desire.

Now I am lost. Lost between right and wrong. I'm in a raging ocean, being tossed to and fro, pulled under where breath escapes me, and I revel in the excitement of newly discovered waters.

I feel as the last leaves of autumn must feel. As the winds of passion blow, I hang on to the morality that keeps me bound in place, though inevitably, I will succumb to the wind that is stronger than I. I will fall.

Many times in my life I've felt trepidation. I have heard the warning bells sounding in my head, telling me danger lies this way. Always before I turned from my path, heeding reason and logic. Always ruled by these things.

For once in my life I welcome the danger though disaster may befall me... Though my landing maybe hard... Though the water drowns me... I seek that which you alone can give. Wild passion. Unbridled lust. A renewed sense of life, and what it means to live it.

Beyond What Was

They were worlds apart,
With no where to start,
Faceless friends in a sea,
Of nameless humanity.
But when he whispered, his love had fled,
Mixed with his own, her tears were shed.

He was Broken...

Wrapped within her wounded pride,
In the dead of night, she quietly cried,
O'er affection that was to her denied,
Though she was a faithful bride.
And when he saw how she lamented,
Words of comfort he submitted.

Broken was She...

Friendship became something more,
When two hearts met so freshly torn.
Brought together by an ageless need,
As life chose to bring them to their knees.
They drew their comfort from each other,

Lending strength one to another,
Their Hearts did Mend...

A love like those from ages past,
One strong, and true, and steadfast,
Born anew from crumbled dreams,
Came to them on trembling wings.
They dared to be so bravely bold,
As to claim a love they could hold.
When offers Fate, Tender in its Keep...

Brought together by mutual need,
She was for him, and her for he,
As they clung with mutual desire,
To what had been born of fire.
Against the odds they played their hand,
They chose their path and made their stand.
A Far Sweeter Destiny...

Cherished Memory

Cherished memory,
From days gone by.
A dream that fades,
With passing of time.
Gone is the little girl,
With stars in her eyes.
Here stands a woman,
That no longer cries.
A woman made hard,
By the realities of life.
Striped of her innocence,
Made strong by its strife.
Gone is the young man,
Who needed me then.
In his place stands a soldier,
Asking, "Do you remember when?"
Yes, my darling,
I most certainly do.
Rare are the days,
I escape thoughts of you.
Your voice a whisper,

Your image a dream,
A thought in my heart,
A memory I can keep.

So Much Left Unspoken

How unexpected life can be.
How useless are our plans?
When only fate has eyes to see,
The cards she intends to hand.
Life moves on whether old or young,
Uncaring of the words we speak,
And of those held upon our tongue,
When cowardice makes us weak.
I thought our union was forever,
Both here and in the life to come.
But suddenly our love you severed,
And in so doing left me undone.
I am lost as to your reason,
For no displeasure have you displayed,
Throughout the long seasons,
And many memories that we've made.
Let me therefore your lips but taste,
So they cannot speak sweet lies.
For whilst I am in your embrace,
Bitter goodbye is held in your eyes.
I pray thee then that thou would turn,

And without backward glance,
Blind mine eyes from what I yearn,
For your image is a pointed lance,
It pierces heart and shatters soul,
Stealing today and all tomorrows,
There is naught left to say, so go,
Leave me to wallow for a time in sorrow.

Blind Eyes Wide Open

How strange it feels to be here now.
My emotions are in a tumult.
So callously I forsook the vows,
That brought me to this place.
Through today's eyes I see and grieve,
Though looking back I regret nothing.
I cannot judge that which I cannot perceive,
And the morals by which I judge are skewed.
Deception breeds more of the same,
Until the day comes you deceive yourself.
Your world crumbles and you're to blame.
Tears count for little and thoughts for less.
Words are lost upon a twisted tongue.
Two steps forward and then you fall.
Tomorrow is gone, and your life has begun.
Or it has ended, depending on the moment.
Searching blindly for what isn't there.
Looking so hard you miss the obvious.
Bravely the consequences, I smile and bare,
Swear to all that ask, this is what I wanted.

Love Unattained

I've lost something to precious to name.
Is the pain less if left in ambiguity?
Can one lament what was never theirs to claim?
Something, just beyond my grasp,
Balanced upon scales of risk and chance,
That tipped against my favor at last,
When fear refused to release my tongue,
And; words failing to make their escape,
Ended what had only begun.

Awaking Desire

I come to you a virgin, not in body, but in soul.
You've loosed my inhibition, so let the passion flow.
You threw embers in a fire, turned my body to a flame,
So I come to you now, without modesty or shame.
Draw close, sweet lover, and press your lips to mine,
Like waves upon the coast, we are destined to collide.
Secrets of the flesh, we will endeavor to explore
Until ecstasy sends us spiraling to Utopian shores.

Stolen

Stolen moments lived anew,
How bitter sweet their end.
For though lived in memory only,
A moment stolen still it is.
The promises of the present,
Take precedence I know.
Still, how desperately I do desire,
To let the past take hold.
Worry not, my precious love;
He, who holds my heart today,
If on occasion the past comes calling,
And for a moment, steals me away.

Where Cruelty Lives

Oil and Water

Hidden meanings behind secreted smiles.
Water over bridges that runs for miles.
Blood like water thin and weak.
Water like blood saturating deep.
Backs with holes and faces fresh.
What a damn mess.
What can't be said actions scream.
Words bellowed that demean.
Righteous anger, justice denied.
Over tears the innocent cried.
Do not e're come to me,
Expecting an apology.
History marked with skeletal bones.
Harsh lies delivered in happy tones.
Gathered together as family,
Ignoring the obvious incompatibilities.
Differences of opinion cannot be fixed.
Oil and water just don't mix.

I'm Not in Your Image

You say you love me, but you don't know who I am.
What you want me to be,
Is really all that you see,
And I'm to the point that I don't give a damn.
I've let you down, and so you've disowned,
What you perceive,
As sin in me.
Yet hell awaits for those who cast the first stone.
I walk in and watch you turn away.
I am the weed,
You'd pluck to be free,
From the shame at my feet you were so quick to lay.
My mother's child, you call me cursed.
My heart bleeds,
But my conscience is clean,
And though sinful, I could be worse.
I'm not in your image, and there's no change of course.
No turn of key,
Nor penalty,
Will place within my breast remorse.
So love me as I am, or not, if you choose.

I desire a peace,
That you cannot bequeath,
And should you rebuke no sleep will I loose.

Betrayal of Blood

I wonder if you know how deep your words cut in.
How foolish to believe love was freely given.
For if you have a heart of stone,
If your conscience can't be found,
If all you do is hurt,
I'd rather you were not around.
I love you…
But your hate runs too deep,
And from my children, I would that hatred keep.
So take your leave, and see to your selfish will,
And though my heart doth break, I will love you still.

Where It Ends

The Ocean Rolls

Rolling shades of blues and greys,
White capped waves break over.
From the sun comes spearing rays,
Till the surface shimmers like glass.
A salty breeze caresses the land,
As ships head towards the harbor.
A storm is brewing by God's own hand.
We stand still while the ocean rolls.

The Wind

Words from your lips depart,
You shutter for you know,
The secrets of your heart,
Waft on the winds that blow.
The chill breeze betrays you,
Sharp as a traitor's knife.
You dared your dreams to pursue,
You dared to live your life.
Clouds roll across a troubled sky,
Revelation like fire falls.
Fury erupts and a storm ignites,
And still you seek destiny's call.
Thunder bellows for all to hear,
Your voice carried upon its wings,
And though encompassed by your fear,
A greater truth doth ring.
Secrets always seek the light,
And wind will always wait,
To cast your dreams into the night,
And what emerges we accept as fate.

Where the World Ends

I have been where the world ends,
Where the ocean kisses the sky,
Where the dolphins play in dancing waves,
And the seagulls swoop and dive.
Where pale pinks and purple hues,
Lazily along the horizon lay,
Until divine shades of perfect blues,
Signals the dawning of a new day.

And Despite What Was

As Her Mother

As her mother you remember:
The day of her birth.
Her invaluable worth.
The first words she said.
The first tears she shed.
As her mother you remember:
School the first day.
Her first friend made.
The fears she couldn't shake.
And her first big mistake.
As her mother you remember:
When she began her own life.
When she became someone's wife.
When her children came along.
When trials made her strong.
As her mother you remember:
When she grew too tired to stand.
When she reached for God's holy hand.
When salvation was given by grace.
When she at last finished the race.

As her mother you can no longer see:
But God has dried her last tear,
Conquered all her fears,
Holds her in the palm of his hand,
Until you can join her in the Promised Land.

Liars Made

In time, they say, the pain will fade,
But they've themselves liars made.
For no such balm have I found,
Since first you slept beneath the ground.
I fear your death has sorrow cast,
And in its shadow grief doth last.
For when each dawn breaks anew,
So does the loss of losing you.

Conclusion

It matters not what life we are born to, but what matters is the life we aspire to. We all have monsters to face. We all have terrors to overcome. Each of us could call ourselves victims, in one way or another, if we so chose, but how much greater to call ourselves survivors.

www.ingramcontent.com/pod-product-compliance
Lightning Source LLC
Chambersburg PA
CBHW020430010526
44118CB00010B/516